ARE YOU READY TO FIGHT

ARE YOU READY TO FIGHT?

The Good Fight of Faith
1 Timothy 6:12

AUTHORS:

JOSEPH L. JOHNSON
AND
JOHN E. JOHNSON

XULON PRESS

Xulon Press
2301 Lucien Way #415
Maitland, FL 32751
407.339.4217
www.xulonpress.com

Foreword by Dr. Gregory.Walker,

Unless otherwise indicated, Scripture quotations taken from the King James Version (KJV)—*public domain.*

Paperback ISBN-13: 978-1-6628-4474-4
Ebook ISBN-13: 978-1-6628-4517-8

TABLE OF CONTENTS

DEDICATION

This book is dedicated to our family who has supported us in this entire project. We want to also acknowledge some family members we have lost along the way Joy, Journey, Cameron and Nakwita (Nikki) and a host of others we love you all and the best is yet to come.

Joseph & John.

FOREWORD

I have had the privilege of seeing and experiencing the spiritual growth and the evolving ministries of this dynamic father and son team, Reverend Joseph L. Johnson, and Reverend John E. Johnson. Like family, we have shared our earthly lives together. God Almighty has had His hand on these kingdom workers throughout life protecting, providing, and preparing them for such a time as this. These two preachers have been shaped, trained, commissioned, and now deployed during world pandemic to carry the Gospel of Jesus Christ. The Holy Spirit has empowered them in this literary work to impact the world. As a preacher, pastor and once prodigal Son I can attest to the fact that within the earthly journey *Spiritual Warfare* is a reality, which will confront every believer and non-believer. However, God did not intend for any of us to contend in spiritual warfare of this life alone. All who profess to live in Christ can live victoriously "…we are more than conquerors…" (See Rom. 8:23). No one must live life complicated by failure and defeat. Satan, the father of all lies and the prince of this world is irritated, always plotting against us, the beloved of Christ Jesus. He seeks to kill, steal, and destroy all (See John 10:10). Satan's agitation is not just with the believers, but Christ living in you! In their work, "**Are You Ready to Fight?**" The authors simplistically share with its readers challenging, informing, equipping us for spiritual battle, and how to succeed as overcomers. Certainly, in this walk called life, we wrestle NOT simply with flesh and blood. We are informed that:

> "For we wrestle not against flesh and blood, but against principalities, against powers, against the rulers of the darkness of this world, against spiritual wickedness in high places." (Eph. 6:12)

In this extraordinary work, the preachers unveil the timeless biblical principles that guide us through the warfare encountered in life. These messengers call attention to the responsibility and accountability of the Church to help those in our churches as well as to meet the needs of those in our greater community. They emphasize the basic human needs of food, clothing, and shelter. The authors sound an urgent alarm to be about The Father's Business. It is a call through two questions! Are you ready to fight a world system? Are you ready to engage in spiritual warfare?

Through biblical instructions the "Christian's Playbook" readers are informed and equipped to begin their journey in spiritual warfare by studying the "Seed" the Word of God and putting on the whole armor of God, so that we can stand!

We fight as Jesus' example, using the Holy Word of God! The writers instruct us to guard our spirits, our hearts, and minds; the places the evil one attacks!

In the book of Matthew, chapter 28 verses 19 to 20, reminds us of Jesus' intention for the called-out body of believers. The Johnson father and son team call the universal church to a unified action, "… to spread the Word, and preach the Word to those who do not know who Christ is and to tell those who do not know what he has done."

This work challenges us, calls, and instructs us for the fight, directing us to victory! I recommend this book! It will aid and prompt intentional strategic actions in the spiritual warfare we all face. Blessings and peace be upon the authors and all that read and employ this work.

Rev. Dr. Gregory Walker, Senior Pastor

Warrensville C. B. Church - Maple Heights, Ohio

D. Min. Advisor Ashland Theological Seminary - Practical
Theology Department

Instructor Ohio Leadership Academy - Cleveland, Ohio

Spiritual Care Southwest General Hospital - Middleburg
Heights, Ohio

CHAPTER 1

Accountability

In the Merriam-Webster Dictionary, the word accountability is best defined as answerable, responsible.

Do not we as the Church, the Ecclesiastical body of Christ, have a responsibility to those in our churches as well as in our communities? People need help, regardless of what political party is in control locally or on a national level; the Church is responsible to meet the needs of the community that is called to serve.

> "Don't be selfish; don't try to impress others. Be humble, thinking of others better than yourselves. Don't look out only for your own interests, but take an interest in others, too."
>
> (Phil. 2:3-4, NLT)

Putting this theory into practice, the authors took the liberty to survey members of the Church and the local community, as we will see in second chapter how they viewed the responsibility of the Church as it relates to being accountable to themselves and others.

In the city where we currently reside, we have seen five hundred or more persons inconveniently forced out of their homes in our same street. These individuals were informed that their homes and/or apartments were infested with asbestos, rats, and roaches to say the least. While this community was being evacuated, they were promised that their place of residence was going to be thoroughly cleaned and fixed to permit them to return to their homes and/or apartments. Unfortunately, that was not the case, instead what was resurrected in that specific area were homes valued over two hundred thousand dollars, which raises the question, how can someone on public assistance afford these new homes? The truth is, some were not able and were displaced all over the city from the community they once knew are now lost in the system and the Church is missing in action.

What about the homeless in Washington Park? From what has been observed, not enough churches are involved to help meet their needs. Then there are others who sleep under the bridges and attempt to protect themselves from the elements by covering their bodies with cardboards, newspapers, or old worn-out covers. These same individuals cannot afford to buy their sustenance and they stand in the street holding up signs stating they will work for food or hoping that a compassionate person will stop to give them a dollar or two. I have been going through my normal routine throughout the day and have observed a homeless man digging through the trash searching for something to satisfy his hunger. In other words, eating our garbage that we carelessly disregard.

Jesus put it this way: "for I was hungry, and you gave me food; I was thirsty, and you gave me something to drink; I was a stranger, or naked, or sick, or in prison, and did not minister unto thee? Jesus answers their question by saying:

"Verily I say unto you, insomuch as ye did it not to
one of the least of these, ye did it not to me."
(Matt. 25:37-45, KJV)

Earlier in the ninth chapter of the book of Matthew, verse
thirty-seven, Jesus is talking to the Church (the disciples) saying,
"The harvest truly is plenteous, but the laborers are few." I do not
know how you feel about this, but most of the time all we see
is our churches in a perpetual motion. Meaning that we like the
idea of or the presentation of going to a physical building Sunday
after Sunday, fifty-two times a year and that is all we are con-
tent in doing.

Furthermore, this elevates questions for us to consider within
ourselves:

When are we going to be about Father's business? Additionally,
when are we going to get out beyond the four walls, meet the
people and their needs, and proselytize them?

Jesus in His great commission gives us all a mandate; He said:

"Go ye therefore, and teach all nations, baptizing
them in the name of the father, and of the son, and
of the Holy Ghost: Teaching them to observe all
things whatsoever I have commanded you: and lo,
I am with you always, even unto the end of the
world. Amen."
(Matt. 28:19, KJV)

Everything we can read about Jesus Christ, you are able to
find that He also met needs of the people and then gave them the
Bread of Life, the Word of God. If you have spent any amount of
time in church at all, then you have heard the story of the feeding
of five thousand. He fed them all with two fish and five loaves

of bread. If you truly read the story, His disciples (the Church) question Him, they asked Him if they could run into town and buy what they needed, but Jesus asked, what do you have? They responded with, two fishes and five loaves of bread? What you and I can gather from this portion of scripture is that He being Jesus sat them down, thanked God, fed their physical body (or met their needs) and from there was about to build up the kingdom of God in other words proselytize them. Accountability is a reality of what Paul said, "That at the name of Jesus every knee shall bow, of things in heaven and things in earth, and things under the earth. In addition, that every tongue should confess that Jesus Christ is Lord, to the glory of God the Father. Can you not see the account-ability in the few lines Paul wrote to the church of Philippi? Just like these words were addressed to the Church back then, they still apply and are even more prevalent today.

In November of 2004, during the time of the Presidential elec-tion, a couple of senior citizens filed a lawsuit, which concerns the right to vote. Several local politicians criticized these individuals for standing up for their civil rights. Which raises the question, when are we going to stop trying to destroy each other's character or have a crab in the bucket type of mentality, pulling each other down when we should only try to do better. What is ironic about this situation is that African Americans were opposing the ones fighting for the rights of others to vote especially for African Americans. Leaving one to wonder if those who were opposing forgot that our ancestors gave their lives so that we might have the right to vote and that they fought to make a correction of the fourteenth amendment. The book of Hebrews defines accountability this way:

> "And let us consider one another in order to stir up
> love and good works, not forsaking the assembling
> of ourselves together, as is the manner of some, but

exhorting one another, and so much the more as
you see the Day approaching."

(Heb. 10:24-25, KJV)

Our readiness to fight starts and ends with our foundation on
the Word of God and allowing it to examine our lives holding us
accountable for our actions, words, and deeds. The question you
and I must ask ourselves at this very moment is, are you ready to
fight and who can hold you accountable as you navigate through
the ring of life?

CHAPTER 2

Is the Church Doing
What it is Called to do?

In the prior chapter, we discussed what accountability appears to be and to understand how we are viewed within and without the four walls. We asked people from various backgrounds and ages for their thoughts to help us see the need to get in the fight.

Survey #1: Is the Church doing what it is called to do?

I do not consider the Church to be doing what it has been called to do. I am being a Christian, feel that the Church (as a whole) is doing what God calls it to do, however, some are not conducting what God has commanded them. As a Christian, you are ordered to spread and preach the Word of God to those whom do not know Christ and share what He has done for you and me that He died on the cross for our sins. If we were to be doing what God calls us to do, then why are we not spreading the Word of God to the communities and advising them that God's word is real. All you must do is trust and believe in the Lord's word. So personally, the Church is doing their part when God calls on the church, yet sometimes we tend to drop the ball when God calls on us to fulfill the Great Commission. (Nikki Ferguson)

Survey # 2: Is the Church doing what it is called to do?

I believe that we as Christians need to step up. There are several individuals not growing in Christ and who are still stuck in a comfort zone. We sometimes use the phrase "God knows my heart," though my question is, do you know your heart and where are you with Christ? Going to church every Sunday is simply not enough. Christians need to learn and study the Word of God. There are many lost souls and back sliders in our neighborhoods and communities, which we are ignoring them by solely concentrating on those within congregations. We need to pray arduously for those who do not know Christ. Secondly, we also need to live model lifestyles that reflect us being Disciples of Christ. In doing so, others will understand something clearly at last shining within us and will want to know the Lord for themselves. Therefore, to answer the question yes, we are doing what we are called to do as the Church and that is spreading the Good News and fulfilling the great commission. (Regina Winston).

Survey # 3 Is the Church doing what it is called to do?

Personally, the Church is not doing what God has called it to do. I can say one thing, what God called the Church to do is to tell others about Him by teaching and preaching the Good News. If the Church were carrying out what God has commanded, there would be more people following Jesus Christ and less in the streets. There would more Christians and less sinners. I am certain there would be more individuals trying to do right and less whom do not care. We would see more love and less hate.

On that account, if the church were doing more of the one thing that I previously mentioned, the world would be in a much better place. (Anonymous)

Survey # 4 Is the Church doing what it is called to do?

I have gone to many churches in my lifetime. When I was young, I was raised Catholic, then I got married and went to a Baptist church. I will say that both denominations suited me. My mom worked for a preacher and his family for over 28 years, and he was a good man though his family were not religious, but in my heart, I am certain that individuals are not to mistreat people even though they claim to be Christian. I was raised to do unto others as you would have them do unto you and I will attempt to stand by that rule.

Currently, it seems like all you hear is negativity coming from the churches. I sometimes consider when a church has a large congregation, they lose sight of what is important, period, as if they do not know your name, or if you have family problems, nor if there are financial problems, etc. smaller churches get to know the people and seem like they are able to often help families through difficult times.

Nonetheless, your congregation is the one that makes the church, though what kills me is that there are people in the church who are deacons, teacher, elders that go out and sin through the week and then on the weekends go to church and pretend that nothing happened. When people who do not belong to a church see this, most think, why should I become a Christian? Many feel that they live a better life than the ones they witness people in the church live. Nowadays everyone desires money in the church and that is fine; I think people should give what they can and not be pressured nor talked down upon by what they give. I know you are supposed to give ten percent, though there are some that cannot offer that. I believe that more members of the Church should go out and visit people and invite them to church, although do not pressure them. I would say there is a great deal that has not ever been asked for currently. I know there are some people in the church that try to run it all and before you know it, the church has been broken apart, so, the Church has room to grow. (Perspective of an average churchgoer)

Survey # 5 Is the Church doing what it is called to do?

To answer your question, one thing that God does not do in his army is draft people. He asks if you want to enlist using the parable about the seed some people believe the word and some people do not believe. Therefore, some people are in the fight even though they may be wounded, others after being wounded quit, and some are just there for a title. (Joel)

This question has been going on for some time now, and we want to continue the conversation and ask the question is the church doing what it called to do? You can ask one hundred people the same question from all types of status both Christian and Non-Christian and a variety of answers can be obtained as you read at the beginning of this chapter. In our hometown of Cincinnati, Ohio, what we have noticed and you as well, in whatever city you reside in, is that in some cases, though not all is that we as the Church can be our own worst enemy. When we allow our denominational affiliations separate us, the role of women in ministry, baptism in the name of Jesus or in the name of the Father, Son, and the Holy Spirit, and a laundry list of other things. Churches fighting in fear because of jealousy, strife, pride, and greed, we must know that the devil wants to keep us divided. Here is how the Apostle Paul address this matter:

"For we wrestle not against flesh and blood, but against principalities, against power, against the rulers of the darkness of this world against spiritual wickedness in high places."

(Eph. 6:12, KJV)

We are fighting against flesh and blood when it is really a spiritual fight.

When we look at the book of John, it states in essence that Jesus was and is praying that we come together as one.

"Neither pray I for these alone, but for them also which shall believe on me through their word; That they all may be one; as thou, Father, art in me, and I in thee, that they also may be one in us: that the world may believe that thou hast sent me. And the glory which thou gavest me I have given them; that they may be one, even as we are one: I in them, and thou in me, that they may be made perfect in one; and that the world may know that thou hast sent me, and hast loved them, as thou hast loved me."

(John 17:20-23, KJV)

There are two important items that are key, first Jesus points out the need for us (the Church) to "be one." It must have been important for Him to mention that we become one. Secondly, that the world may know that there is no division in the church. He says: "...Every kingdom divided against itself is brought to desolation; and every city or house divided against itself shall not stand." (Matt.12:25b, KJV) The devil already knows that when we (the Church) come together as the Word of God says: "There is one body and one Spirit, just as you also were called in one hope of your calling." (Eph. 4:4, KJV) Christ empowers us with his power and the good news is that the devil had been defeated. Spiritual warfare has been going on since the beginning of time according to the bible. If we examine the book of Genesis 3, Adam and Eve were in a spiritual battle.

The bible says:

> "Be sober be vigilant because your adversary the devil as a roaring lion walketh about, seeking whom he may devour."
>
> (1 Pt. 5:8, KJV)

Two key words: **sober** and **vigilant**.

Sober: in this biblical context means to be calm and collected in spirit.

Vigilant: in this biblical context means to watch, give strict attention to be cautious.

When in spiritual warfare we need to put on the whole armor of God so that we can stand against the tricks of the devil (adversary). God's armor is not optional when it comes to spiritual warfare. It is imperative that we face the enemy in the strength of our lord and savior Jesus Christ. Remember even though Christ has been victorious in defeating the devil we are still called to stand and face the enemy assaults with the armor of God and assault the enemy with the Sword of the Spirit, which is the word of God. Paul reminds us that during the time when he was authoring the book of Ephesians, he saw the Roman soldiers outside of his prison cell. The Roman helmet was made of bronze, or leather or a combination of the two to protect their head from deadly blows, God requires us to do the same thing.

The helmet of salvation deals with the mind! At salvation, we repent, or we turn from sin and turn to Christ as our savior. In the Greek, the word for repent is a compound word that comes from a word that means change, and a word that means mind. Sin separated us from God, but the Holy Spirit is whom convicts us of our sin that separates us from God. As we believe Jesus and confess Him as Lord, then we receive a new mindset. Here is what Paul says:

> "Because the carnal mind is enmity against God;
> for it is not subject to the law of God, neither
> indeed can be."
>
> (Rom. 8:7, KJV)

In other words, the carnal mind is at war with God. Today people are overwhelmed in their minds, with depression, Attention Deficit Disorder (ADD), loneliness, and low self-esteem, which can be negative words others may say about you and can put you and I in a state of depression. The devil will do any and everything he can; he will whisper words of discouragement in our ears. His job is to put us in the position of Eve. To be moved by our own feelings and emotions rather than the truth of the Word of God.

We need the helmet of salvation and the sword of the Spirit, which is the Word of God as a covering and a protection for our minds to deflect and defeat the adversary with all his schemes. The bible says:

> "But let us, who are of the day, be sober, putting
> on the breastplate of the faith, and love; and for a
> helmet, the hope of salvation."
>
> (1 Thess. 5:8, KJV)

The devil would love to discourage us in our hope; we are to encourage and edify one another, to lift one another up when we are discouraged. Whose report will you believe?

If we are going to be successful in this spiritual battle, our warfare must be waged according to the Scriptures. In the sports world, take football for example, you are given a playbook to study and learn the plays for your team, the route, and or your responsibilities during that play. When it comes to playing against your opposition, the team will have a film session to watch their opponent's plays, so that they can be prepared to the best of their ability when facing them. At times, you may have been able to get a playbook used by the opposing team. Now when we consider God our heavenly coach¹, He wrote the Christians a playbook. Our playbook is the Bible. Just as football players must study their playbook, we have an obligation to study ours. In the book of second Timothy chapter 2 verse fifteen, tells us to study the Word of God, show ourselves approved unto God a workman that does not need to be ashamed and rightly divide the word of truth. When we study the Word of God (playbook), we will discover what our opposition is doing.

The playbook says, that the devil is a roaring lion, walking around looking for someone to devour (See 1 Pet. 5:8). The playbook states, there is no truth in him, he is the father of lies (See John 8:44). The playbook says that he is the accuser of the brethren (See Rev. 12:10).

The key is: we overcome him by the blood of the lamb and the word of our testimony (See Rev. 12:11) The playbook says, he will come as the false Christ and false prophets, they will raise, they will show signs and wonders to seduce if it were possible, even the elect. (See Mark 13:22)

The playbook also shows us how to beat our opposition: Jesus shows us how in fourth chapter of Matthew verses 1 through 11, there are three key words "It is written" then verse eleven says the devil left him alone. The playbook says: "Submit yourselves therefore to God. Resist the devil, and he will flee from you." (James 4:7, KJV) Again, the playbook says, "Nay, in all these things we are more than conquers through Him that loved us." (Rom. 8:37, KJV)

The playbook reiterates that we are of God and have overcome them "…because greater is he that is in you, than he that is in the world." (1 John 4:4b, KJV) The playbook tells us that we win:

> "And the devil that deceived them was cast into the
> lake of the fire and brimstone, where the beast and
> the false prophet are, and shall be tormented day
> and night forever and ever."
>
> (Rev. 20:10, KJV)

Then Christ goes on to say:

> "And, behold, I come quickly; and my reward is
> with me, to give every man according as his work
> shall be."
>
> (Rev. 22:12, KJV)

Victory, victory we have the victory. Satan's armor (strongholds) will be removed and destroyed as well as his teammates.

CHAPTER 3

How is your Heart?

Some years ago, early on in my ministry, I (Joseph) preached a sermon entitled "Decorated Tombstone." In addition, I never knew how rhetorical those words were until now. Some twenty years later. (Rhetorical means, speaking or writing effectively). You see that some two thousand years ago Jesus Christ the Messiah wrote these very profound words to the church when He said:

(Decorated Tombstone) "Woe unto you, scribes and Pharisees, hypocrites! for ye make clean the outside of the cup and of the platter, but within they are full of extortion excess. Thou blind Pharisee, cleanse first that which is within the cup and platter, that the outside of them may be clean also. Woe unto you, scribes and Pharisees, hypocrites! for ye are like unto whited sepulchers, which indeed appear beautiful outward, but within are full of dead men's bones, and of all uncleanness. Even so, ye also outwardly appear

righteous unto men, but within ye are full
of hypocrisy and iniquity."

(Matt. 23:25-28, KJV)

Accordingly, it seems to me, that our Lord and Savior was talking to us the redeemed the household of faith, we who have been washed in His Blood. Those who dress up each Sunday, talk all the church talk. You know what I mean praise the Lord, God is a good God, Hallelujah, glory to His Name etc. Singing in the choir, stand at the doors and usher, preach in the pulpits and they are your Deacon and Deaconess, and those who sit in the pew.

Nonetheless, let me say this, it is not everybody but one or two that can put an indictment on the church. I said this because, too many times I have seen people come to church with their INFIRMITY and I have noticed that the Church those "SCRIBES and PHARISEES" who look good on the outside. Men can look good on the outside, because men look at the outward appearance, they only see the three-piece suits and nice shoes, women in their church attire, our kids in their attire, though, the inside where the heart is, nothing but dead men bones, in other words, "DECORATED TOMBSTONES."

Jesus said, "For where your treasure is, there will your heart be also." (Matt. 6:21) We have become too materialistic instead of Spiritualistic concern about the outside then the inside. We are Eccentric in our behavior we got off the path that God has set for us. You remember the words of Solomon in the book of Proverbs, "In all thy ways acknowledge him, and he shall direct thy paths." (Prov. 3:6, KJV)WHOSE DIRECTION ARE YOU FOLLOWING?

Today some twenty-six years later I just happen to be reading in the book of Luke, chapter 8, verses1 through15, the parable of the Sower a familiar story in the scriptures. Jesus talks about a farmer sowing seed. He had His twelve disciples with Him, a certain woman who had been healed of evil spirits and infirmities Mary Magdalene who had seven devils, Joanna, and Susanna they ministered unto Him with their substance! Many other people had also gathered to hear Jesus speak on this parable. Jesus spoke these words:

> "A Sower went out to sow his seed: and as he sowed
> some fell by the way side; and it was trodden down,
> and the fowls of the air devoured it. And some fell
> upon a rock; and as soon as it was sprung up, it
> withered away, because it lacked moisture, And
> some fell among thorns; and the thorns sprang
> up with it, and choked it. And other fell on good
> ground, and sprang up, and bare fruit a hundred-
> fold. And when he had said these things, he cried,
> He that hath ears to hear, let him hear."
>
> (Luke 8:5-8, KJV)

Even so, His disciples did not understand what Jesus was referring to in the ninth verse of the same chapter of the book of Luke, "And his disciples asked him, saying, what might this parable be? (KJV) Moving forward, in verse eleven, Jesus explained the parable. (Jesus never left them without an explanation).

> "Now the parable is this: The seed is the Word of
> God. Those by the way side are they that hear; then
> cometh the devil, and taketh away the word out of
> their hearts, lest they should believe and be saved.
> They on the rock, which, when they hear, receive
> the word with joy; and these have not root, which
> for a while believe, and in time of temptation fall

away. And that which fell among thorns are they, which, when they have heard, go forth, and are choked with cares and riches and pleasures of this life, and bring no fruit to perfection. But that on the good ground are they, which in an honest and good heart, having heard the word, keep it, and bring forth fruit with patience."

(Luke 8:11-15, KJV)

To cultivate our hearts, we must allow God's word to plow it up, in other words, our hearts, minds, and souls giving complete control over to God. We must ask God to break up the hard rocky surface of our hearts and turn over the bitterness, un-forgiveness that has made us unproductive and useless for the work he wants you to do. "YOU HAVE NOT BECAUSE YOU ASK NOT!" After you have allowed the word of God to break up the hollow ground then there must be some "fertilization." For this process to work, you must spend time in the Word of God. Spending time is not reading your bible just on Sunday. You must go into your quiet room, wherever that may be, and really get into the Word and the Word get into you, allowing it to soak deep into your heart and watch the word change your life.

As God told Joshua to meditate day and night so that His truth can saturate our minds, souls, and hearts. God's word will permeate our thoughts and our conversation as well as how we treat others. Have you ever washed dishes before, and soap is still in the glass? The only way to get all the soap out is to run fresh water continually in the glass and allow the water to push the soap out until all you see is clear water. So then meditating on the scripture the word of God then allowing the Holy Spirt to be the water you and I need to clean out all the junk inside of us.

So then, after the fertilization you must apply the truth of the Bible to take place in our lives and do what it says. Remember we are commanded to be not only hearers of the word only, but a doer as well. That is if you want a HARVEST. Nevertheless, to see a harvest you must weed the garden off your heart. You must guard your heart protect it from the thorns of anxiety and the worry of this world so that you might be about our Fathers business. On His sermon on the mount, Jesus told those who were to, "But seek first the kingdom of God, and His righteousness; and all these things shall be added unto you." (Matt. 6:33, KJV) Ask yourself, how is your Heart? Life itself flows through the Heart.

Diagram
Circulating Blood

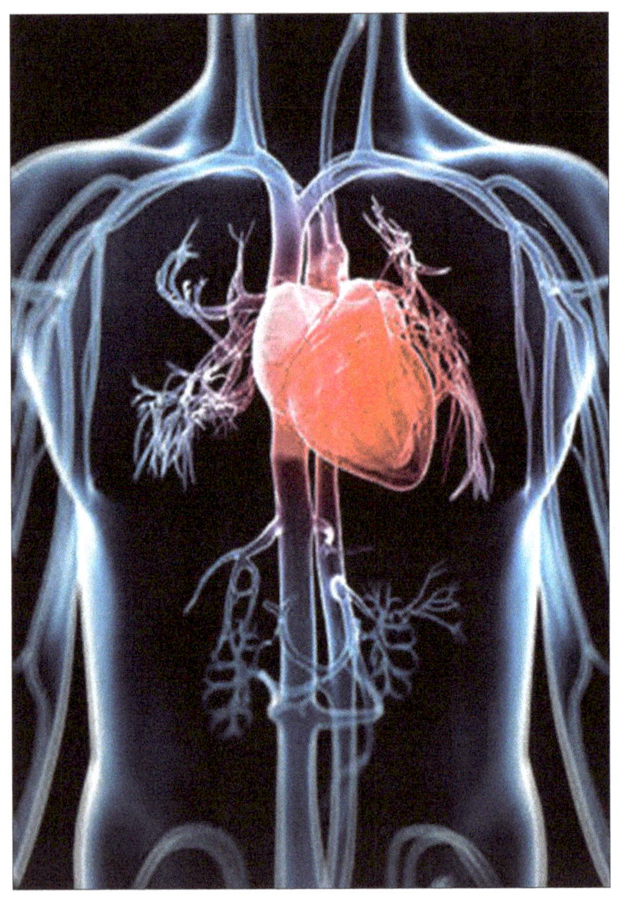

The steady pumping of the heart supports life by moving blood through the body. As it flows, blood delivers food and oxygen to all the body's cells and carries away wastes. Blood returns to the heart carrying a waste gas called carbon dioxide that cells produce as they use oxygen to obtain energy from food. Blood carrying carbon dioxide enters that right atrium through the superior vena cava and inferior vena cava. That atrium then contracts, squeezing the blood through the tricuspid valve into the right ventricle. After that ventricle fills, pressure forces the tricuspid valve to close and the pulmonic valve, leading to the pulmonary artery, to open. That ventricle then contracts, and the blood-gushes through the pulmonary artery into the lungs. In the lungs, the blood releases carbon dioxide and picks up oxygen. Oxygenated blood from the lungs travels to the left atrium. ("biology chapter 18- test 3 - BIOL 1112 ... - Course Hero") That atrium then contracts, which squeezes the blood through the mitral valve into the left ventricle. "After blood fills the ventricle, the mitral valve closes, and the aortic valve opens." ("www.hik-consulting.pl/edu Single Channel ECG Telemetry ...") Blood pours into the aorta and flows through arteries to bring oxygen to the body.

CHAPTER 4

Our Faith is Being Challenged

I do not know if you know this or if anybody has told you but Satan is a liar and the father of lies. Satan will do his best not only to hinder Gods work but will try to stop you as well. The bible also tells us that Satan will change God's truth and will have you worshiping what has been created rather than the CREATOR Himself, according to first chapter of the book of Romans, verse twenty-five.

The Gospel of Mathew shed light on that central facet:

(WORD) "Then was Jesus led up of the Spirit into the wilderness to be tempted of the devil. And when he had fasted forty days and forty nights, he was afterward an hungered. And when the tempter came to him, he said, If thou be the Son of God, command that these stones be made bread. But he answered and said, It is written, Man shall not live by bread alone, but by every word that proceedeth out of the mouth of

(DOUBT) God. Then the devil taketh him up into the holy city, and setteth him on a pinnacle of the temple, And saith unto him, if thou be the Son of God, cast thyself down: for it is written, He shall give his angels charge concerning thee: and in their hands they shall bear thee up, lest at any time thou *(DOUBT)* dash thy foot against a stone. Jesus said unto him, it is written again, thou shalt not tempt the Lord thy God. Again, the devil *(WORD)* taketh him up into an exceeding high mountain, and sheweth him all the king- *(DOUBT/LIE)* doms of the world, and the glory of them; And saith unto him, all these things will I give thee, if thou wilt fall down and wor- ship me. Then saith Jesus unto him, get *(WORD)* thee hence, Satan: for it is written, thou shalt worship the Lord thy God, and him *(WORD)* only shalt thou serve. Then the devil *(SATAN* leaveth him, and, behold, angels came and *DEFEATED)* ministered unto him."

(Matt. 4:1-11, KJV)

"Submit yourselves therefore to God. Resist the devil, and he will flee from you." (James 4:7, KJV)
Here are important KEYS for all BELIEVERS:

1. Submit to God
2. Resist the devil
3. YOU WILL HAVE THE VICTORY

Listen, everyday our faith is being challenged, through different mediums such as the local and national news, T.V. and radio or social media filled with aggressive assaults about what God has said in His Word. Just for a moment, can we take a small commercial break and examine the difference between what the world says and what God says.

The world says, Jesus is not real and is not the son of God. However, God says:

> "If I have told you earthly things, and ye believe not, how shall ye believe, if I tell you of heavenly things? And no man hath ascended up to heaven, but he that came down from heaven, even the Son of man which is in heaven. And as Moses lifted up the serpent in the wilderness, even so must the Son of man be lifted up: That whosoever believeth in him should not perish, but have eternal life. For God so loved the world, that he gave his only begotten Son, that whosoever believeth in him should not perish, but have everlasting life. For God sent not his Son into the world to condemn the world; but that the world through him might be saved. He that believeth on him is not condemned: but he that believeth not is condemned already, because he hath not believed in the name of the only begotten Son of God."
>
> (John 3:12-18, KJV)

The world says, why would God let this happen? However, God says: "The heart is deceitful above all things, and desperately wicked: who can know it?" (Jer. 17:9, KJV) The Word of God goes on to say, "He that is soon angry dealeth foolishly: and a man of wicked devices is hated." (Prov. 14:17, KJV)

"For from within, out of the heart of men, proceed evil thoughts, adulteries, fornications, murders,

(Mark 7:21, KJV)

"Because that, when they knew God, they glorified him not as God, neither were thankful; but became vain in their imaginations, and their foolish heart was darkened."

(Rom. 1:21, KJV)

"As it is written, There is none righteous, no, not one: There is none that understandeth, there is none that seeketh after God. They are all gone out of the way, they are together become unprofitable; there is none that doeth good, no, not one. Their throat is an open sepulchre; with their tongues they have used deceit; the poison of asps is under their lips: Whose mouth is full of cursing and bitterness: Their feet are swift to shed blood: Destruction and misery are in their ways: And the way of peace have they not known: There is no fear of God before their eyes."

(Rom. 3:10-18, KJV)

The world says to remove prayer; however, God says:

"If my people, which are called by my name, shall humble themselves, and pray, and seek my face, and turn from their wicked ways; then will I hear from heaven, and will forgive their sin, and will heal their land."

(2 Chron. 7:14, KJV)

The Word of God goes on to further state, "And he spake a parable unto them to this end, that men ought always to pray, and not to faint;" (Luke 18:1, KJV) In addition to, "Pray without ceasing." (1 Thess. 5:17, KJV)

We must stop camouflaging whom we are as believers or conforming to the world, stand on the Word of God and speak truth. Power plant the seeds of life and allow God to move on the hearts of people. Today we see many substitutions, Nylon has been substituted for silk, Oleomargarine has been substituted for butter, and Splenda has been substituted for sugar. God insist that we "…keep himself unspotted from the world." (James 1:27b, KJV). Why? Because when a Christian tries to become something or someone else, they lose the essence of whom they really are. Back in 2004, the movie Fat Albert came out and during the movie the character Rudi tells Fat Albert and the rest of their friends that they are not of this world. Those words should resonate with every believer who reads this book, "WE ARE NOT OF THIS WORLD." God puts it the following way in the book of first Kings of the 18th chapter:

"And Elijah came unto all the people, and said, How long halt ye between two opinions? If the Lord be God, follow him: but if Baal, then follow him. And the people answered him not a word."

(1 Kings 18:21, KJV)

We are not too far off from where Elijah was located, the opposing was:

> "Now therefore send, and gather to me all Israel
> unto mount Carmel, and the prophets of Baal four
> hundred and fifty, and the prophets of the groves
> four hundred, which eat at Jezebel's table."
>
> (1 Kings 18:19, KJV)

Elijah faced 850 prophets, all he was asking the people of his time, whose characteristics are you partaking of? Baal (Satan) or God?

Baal (Satan) a liar from the beginning, an accuser of the brethren, a fallen angel, a deceiver, murderer, thief, an enemy of God, and an enslaver. God, the giver of life, a forgiver of sin, friend of sinners, truth, a freedom fighter, a giver of peace, joy, love, meekness, faith, holiness, He is a God of reconciliation, hope for the hopeless, healer, shelter in a storm. He is our Breastplate of righteousness, a supplier of our needs, a righteous judge; He is the captain of our salvation. He is our high priest, the most high God, our tower of refuge, the lifter of our heads, the Good Shepherd.

Just as Joshua called together the people of God in his day, we call the people of God of our day to:

> "And if it seem evil unto you to serve the Lord,
> choose you this day whom ye will serve; whether
> the gods which your fathers served that were
> on the other side of the flood, or the gods of the
> Amorites, in whose land ye dwell; but as for me
> and my house we will serve the Lord."
>
> (Josh. 24:15, KJV)

For an added benefit, read the book by Dr. Leroy Thompson Sr. called, "What to do When Your Faith is Challenged."

<u>Scripture on Faith being CHALLENGED!</u>

Nehemiah 4:1-9	Do not be distracted from your faith.
Nehemiah 6:5-12	Your enemy will not give up so easily, so do not you give up.
I Kings 18:1-39	Faith challenge.
Joshua 6:1-20	Just hold on.
Joshua 1:3	It is yours.
Exodus 14:1-31	Fear not, stand still, and see.
1 Timothy 6:12	Encourage others.

The Word of God goes on to say, "Jesus Christ the same yesterday, and to day, and for ever" (Heb. 13:8, KJV)

CHAPTER 5

The Christian Hall of Fame

The word fame is used because it means REKNOWN and renown means a state of being widely acclaimed and honored. (Webster's dictionary) In New York, they have a building named The Hall of Fame for Great Americans. In that building there are spaces for 102 bronze bust of persons elected to the Hall of Fame. Some of the honorary are Henry W Longfellow, Eli Whitney, Robert Fulton (1900) Harriet Beecher Stowe, and Andrew Jackson (1910). Just as there are other Halls of Fames such as The Hall of Immortals and the Hall of Murals in the International college of Surgeons commemorate great surgeons and scientists. The Hall of Fame for Distribution honors those who have contributed significantly to distribution of goods. Here in Ohio, we have the National Football Hall of Fame and in our hometown of Cincinnati, we have the Cincinnati Reds baseball Hall of fame located downtown at the Great American Ball Park.

As believers, we have the Christian Hall of Fame, and our Hall of Fame is and will be filled with those who have contributed significantly to the Kingdom of God.

Our Hall of Fame is found in Hebrews chapter 11, where it says:

"By faith Abel offered unto God a more excellent sacrifice than Cain, by which he obtained witness that he was righteous, God testifying of his gifts: and by it he being dead yet speaketh. By faith Enoch was translated that he should not see death; and was not found, because God had translated him: for before his translation he had this testimony, that he pleased God. But without faith it is impossible to please him: for he, that cometh to God must believe that he is, and that he is a rewarder of them that diligently seek him. By faith Noah, being warned of God of things not seen as yet, moved with fear, prepared an ark to the saving of his house; by the which he condemned the world, and became heir of the righteousness which is by faith. By faith Abraham, when he was called to go out into a place which he should after receive for an inheritance, obeyed; and he went out, not knowing whither he went. By faith he sojourned in the land of promise, as in a strange country, dwelling in tabernacles with Isaac and Jacob, the heirs with him of the same promise: For he looked for a city which hath foundations, whose builder and maker is God. Through faith also Sara herself received strength to conceive seed, and was delivered of a child when she was past age, because she judged him faithful who had promised. By faith Abraham, when he was tried, offered up Isaac: and he that had received the promises offered up his only begotten son, By faith Isaac blessed Jacob and Esau concerning things to come. By faith Jacob, when he was a dying, blessed both the sons of Joseph; and worshipped, leaning upon the top of his staff. By faith Joseph, when he died, made mention of the departing of the children of Israel; and gave commandment concerning his bones. By faith Moses, when he was born, was hid three months of his parents, because they saw he was a proper child; and they were not afraid of the king's commandment. By faith Moses, when he was come to years, refused to be called the son of Pharaoh's daughter;"

(Heb. 11:4-24, KJV)

The only way for us as believers to enter this Christian Hall of Fame is through your Faith in Jesus and what He has said in His Word. First, understand that Faith is unquestioning belief in God, or complete trust or confidence in Him. Imagine if you will, we are walking into a service at a church, and you go to take your seat what you and I have demonstrated is an act of faith. Someone maybe asking the question, what do you mean my faith is being demonstrated? Whenever we have attended any type of service, we have never seen anyone get down on the floor to see if the pew is still stable enough to hold them, people just sit down trusting that the pew will function as if it was designed to do. When it comes to our Faith in the Lord Jesus Christ, we must trust him. If we have enough faith to sit on pews in some cases that have not been changed or worked on in years to hold us up week in and week up without question. What would your circumstances if you put just as much trust in Him week in and week out with no questions look like. Guess what it does not matter what you are going though He already knows about, not only does he know about but also, He has already worked it out for your good. Let me remind us of what he has already told us in His word.

"Humble yourselves therefore under the mighty hand of God, that he may exalt you in due time: Casting all your care upon him; for he careth for you. Be sober, be vigilant; because your adversary the devil, as a roaring lion, walketh about, seeking whom he may devour: Whom resist stedfast in the faith, knowing that the same afflictions are accomplished in your brethren that are in the world. But the God of all grace, who hath called us unto his eternal glory by Christ Jesus, after that ye have suffered a while, make you perfect, stablish, strengthen, settle you. To him be glory and dominion for ever and ever. Amen."

(1 Pet. 5:6-11, KJV)

However,, if you go a couple of books in the bible to Romans chapter 8, He tells us:

"And we know that all things work together for good to them that love God, to them who are the called according to his purpose. For whom he did foreknow, he also did predestinate to be conformed to the image of his Son, that he might be the firstborn among many brethren. Moreover whom he did predestinate, them he also called: and whom he called, them he also justified: and whom he justified, them he also glorified. What shall we then say to these things? If God be for us, who can be against us?"

(Rom. 8:28-31, KJV)

Listen whatever you are facing give it over to God and know without any doubt He can take care of it and at the same time take care of you. If we have breath in our bodies, we will face all kinds of situations good, bad, or downright ugly, we have enough history with God to carry us through. How so you might ask? This is not the first time you have been sick, dealt with heartache, frustration, out of work, no money, trying to get by, without transportation, the same God who kept you then is the same God who is with you now. While our circumstances and obstacles may change the one thing that is consistent is our God because he is the same yesterday, today and forever meaning your past is covered, your present is covered, and your tomorrow is covered. Once again, "Faith is grasping the unrealities of hope and bringing them into the realm of reality," remember my dear friend, it is the heart of faith that receives from God. (See Mark 11:23-24)

CHAPTER 6

Work to be Done!

In his first book with the help of the Holy Spirit, my Co-Author Joseph asked this profound question, which happens to be the title of the book "What's in your Heart? The whole premise of the book was to get the Body of Christ, the household of faith energized, and motivated to carry out the great commission that our Lord told us to do. Jesus said:

> "Go ye therefore, and teach all nations, baptizing
> them in the name of the Father, and of the Son,
> and of the Holy Ghost: Teaching them to observe
> all things whatsoever I have commanded you: and,
> lo, I am with you always, even unto the end of the
> world. Amen."
>
> (Matthew 28:19-20, KJV)

Most of the time when someone who holds a position of authority when they give and command or directive they will sit back and watch you do the work. But notice what Jesus said, He tells them to Go, Teach, and Baptize but the key factor in doing all of that is lets the believer know that He will be with them always even until the end.

This is a contrast difference in what the world does and says then what Jesus says. In the world, those who have authority to command you to do something do it because they can manipulate someone else or because their ego is driving them. When we allow our ego to take control, we **E**ase **G**od **O**ut.

Please note that not all churches have become complacence, but not enough churches are doing what has been commanded of them. The writer of the book of Matthew in the Word of God in chapter 6, verse twenty-one says, "For where your treasure is, there will your heart be also." (KJV) As the blood brought church of God, we cannot afford to ignore His words. However,, must affirm the word of God as recorded:

> "And the lord said unto the servant, Go out
> into the highways and hedges, and compel
> them to come in, that my house may be filled."
>
> (Luke 14:23, KJV)

(Dunamis-Power)
(Your home first)
(then outside the neighborhood)

> "But ye shall receive power, after that the
> Holy Ghost is come upon you: and ye shall
> be witnesses unto me both in Jerusalem, and
> in all Judea, and in Samaria, and unto the
> uttermost part of the earth.
>
> (Acts 1:8, KJV)

(Your neighborhood)

In trying not to sound negative but what has been observed in some cases the church has been shaken but not stirred. Here is what we mean, there is some things that have "shaken the church" (disturb or cause discomfort) but, not stirred up enough to "Go" out and address these issues. Such as a thirteen-year-old girl stabbing another girl here in our city over the weekend.

Two teenagers of fourteen and fifteen years old, along with three adults have been charged with running a hit for hire ring and have been linked with killing multiple people. The count keeps rising, at the time of writing this; two more homicides had been linked to them bringing the total up to nine killings and a possibility of more as the investigation continues. A fifteen-year-old was sentenced to 50 years to life in prison after he was found guilty of killing two fellow students and wounding thirteen others. Then there was a thirteen-year-old who killed his English teacher on the last day of school and is now serving a 28-year sentence.

The tragedy of each one of these is that cases had some form of influence that was not conducive to their behavior. Paul reminds that even though we may have not committed the acts that they have we have all have one thing in common and that is sin. Paul goes on to say, "For all have sinned, and come short of the glory of God;" (Rom. 3:23, KJV) in other words that may not have been your sin but none of is exempt from sin.

Shaking will not necessarily stir some people, again shaking only will cause discontent and uneasiness if your wellbeing disappointment and disapproval but you notice the shakers will become the movers. Additionally, we become movers by the Holy Ghost. Peter said:

> "For the prophecy came and not in old time by the
> will of man: but holy men of God spake as they
> were moved by the Holy Ghost."
>
> (2 Pet. 1:21, KJV)

Not only did they speak but also had power, (*Dunamis-Power*) to turn world upside down. We should not focus on the trivial things when God has called us to move mountains. Why should we sit in the bathtub when God has called us to part the red seas of life? Why should we focus on the rafts of life when God has called us to build his ark? God is calling us to move into dimensions we never experienced before. So let us Go, seek, and save the lost, bringing them into a dimension they have never experienced before. Let us be like the church of Philadelphia as recorded in the third chapter of the book of Revelation. "The faithful Church." Therefore, when He returns, we will hear him say:

> "His lord said unto him, Well done, good and faithful servant; thou hast been faithful over a few things, I will make thee ruler over many things: enter thou into the joy of thy lord."
>
> (Matt. 25:23, KJV).

CHAPTER 7

A Fighter's Analogy

My father Joseph tells the story of him joining a boxing club with some of his friends he went to school with. When he was younger, at one of the local recreation centers, he had the opportunity to work with fighters such as Greg Lewis, Johnny North, and sometimes Richard Richerson.

One of the trainers at the recreation center was man named Mr. Joiner, and he would have them sparring with one another throwing hooks, jabs, upper cuts, or any combination so that when fight time came, they did not have to guess what punches to throw to defeat their opponent or knock them out. Mr. Joiner had a son named Billy who had one of the greatest opportunities in the world a chance to fight Muhammad Ali. What was so interesting about Ali was his development of the Ali shuffle and the Rope-a-dope. The Ali shuffle would baffle the opponent so much so that in their frustration would lose sight of their fight plan and Ali would batter them with repeated blows. Then when Ali wanted to frustrate them even more, he then would go into the Rope-a-dope in which he would lay on the ropes and allow his opponent to throw all types of punches wearing themselves out, allowing him to take advantage of the situation and the fight and usually win.

Nonetheless, before he reached the stage in the field of boxing. He first had to have the desire to fight. Followed by dieting and exercise to prepare for the upcoming event.

The only way to become the unquestionable undisputed Heavyweight champion of the world was his commitment to training. You could not train one week and then show up next month or even next year to become world champion, no there must be some consistency in the training process. That training consists of hitting the speed bag, heavy bag, jumping rope, running several miles, medicine ball; sit ups, pushups, and sparring. Consistency-consistency-consistency is the name of the game.

Sequentially there are several different weight classes in boxing; see the following listed below:

Heavyweight	200lbs +
Light Heavyweigh	168lbs-175lbs
Middleweight	154lbs-160lbs
Welterweight	140lbs-147lbs
Lightweight	130lbs-135lbs
Featherweight	122lbs-126lbs
Bantamweight	115lbs-118lbs
Flyweight	108lbs-112lbs

Each of these weight limits had or still have their world champion. However, every now then you would have that individual who is considered as punch drunk. Someone who has been impaired by the number of punches they have taken to the head.

Just as there is physical boxing, there is spiritual boxing. We have our Heavyweight, Lightweight, Middleweight, Featherweight,

Bantamweight, and Flyweight divisions, which lets us know we all have a division we can fight.

Here are some Scriptures that states a difference in the way that we as believers in Jesus Christ fight. In the physical area, the two opponents square off against one another in the boxing ring and throw punch after punch until one corner admits defeat or there is a unanimous decision, or even a knockout. There must be physical altercation. As a result, when we read in the bible where God's fighter does not even lift a hand. Let us consider what the Lord said in the book of Exodus: "The Lord shall fight for you, and ye shall hold your peace." (Ex. 14:14, KJV) In the book of first Samuel, it says:

> "That we also may be like all the nations; and that
> our King may judge us, and go out before us, and
> fight our battles."
>
> (1 Sam. 8:20, KJV)

Nehemiah told the people of Israel, no matter what Sanballat said, he cannot stop us, we will defeat what our opponent says and what he does.

> "In what place therefore ye hear the sound of the
> trumpet, resort ye thither unto us: our God shall
> fight for us."
>
> (Neh. 4:20, KJV)

Please remember David's prayer if you will when he said:

> "Plead my cause, O Lord, with them that strive with
> me: fight against them that fight against me."
>
> (Ps. 35:1, KJV)

Just as Paul reminded in the sixth chapter of first book of Timothy in the New Testament:

> "Fight the good fight of faith, lay hold on eternal
> life, whereunto thou art also called, and hast pro-
> fessed a good profession before many witnesses."
>
> (1 Tim. 6:12, KJV)

Listen, everything we do as God's children and as Christians is based on our faith in what God said to all of us through his Word. To remind you in the physical area of boxing (fighting) the two-opponents had to encounter one another to declare a champion. Again, we read where God told Jehoshaphat that I (God) know that you are a great warrior, I know you defeated a number of opponents, but here is what I want you to tell the congregation of Israel and I want to remind you as well.

> "And he said, Hearken ye, all Judah, and
> ye inhabitants of Jerusalem, and thou king
> Jehoshaphat, Thus saith the Lord unto you,
> *(or* Be not afraid nor dismayed by reason of this
> *your opponent)* great multitude; for the Battle is not yours,
> but God's."
>
> (2 Chron. 20:15, KJV)

To prove that we have the Greatest Champion in the history of the Fight Game: some two thousand years ago there was a championship fight. The two opponents consist of Jesus and Satan. Well, the Friday when the first round took place Satan threw a punch that had the believer doubtful that Jesus would recover, and then in the second round (on Saturday) Satan threw a right jab and a couple of combinations and Jesus went down again, and it seemed as if there was no hope for the hopeless.

Knowing that there was a temporary vacated championship. However, in the third round (third day) there was a clash of the Titans. The crowds of those in hell began to cheer their fighter on, just one more blow to the kidney, one more punch to the head; we predicted you would win Satan in the third round, which is what the hell hounds thought.

Nonetheless, Paul interjected with what is listed next:

> "O death, where is thy sting? O grave, where is thy victory?" The sting of death is sin; and the strength of sin is the law. But thanks be to God, which giveth us the victory through our Lord Jesus Christ. We must be steadfast, unmovable, always abounding in the work of Lord, forasmuch as ye know that our labor is not in vain in the Lord."
>
> (1 Cor. 15:55-58, KJV)

Even though Satan looked like he is winning, do not give up. Because early on the third day there was a unanimous decision. The undisputed champion of the world rose from the grave with all the power in His heaven and earth in His hands.

Our King is back on the throne in all His glory, who did not leave us alone to fight the opponent our enemy; He left us with the Word of God. If we want to win, we must:

> "Study to shew thyself approved unto God, a workman that needeth not to be ashamed, rightly dividing the word of truth."
>
> (2 Tim. 2:15, KJV)

All of us are training through Sunday school, bible study, prayer, fasting, to defeat our opponent; there must be consistency and conformity with prior practice and principle. We can no longer be weekend warriors thinking Sunday service will just do it. We must buckle down become consistent in our walk and train our spirit daily to fight.

Scriptures on the word
fight, fighting, fought, and fighteth.

Exodus 1:10; 14:14, 25; 17:9

Deuteronomy 1:30, 41-42; 2:32; 3:22; 20:4, 10

Joshua 9:2; 10:25; 11:5; 19:47; 23:10

Judges 1:1, 3, 9; 8:1; 9:38; 10:9, 18; 11:6, 8, 9, 12, 25, 32; 12:1, 3; 20:20

1 Samuel 4:9; 8:20; 13:5; 15:18; 17:9-10, 19-20, 32-33; 18:17; 23:1; 28:1; 29:8; 25:28

2 Samuel 11:20

1 Kings 12:21, 24; 20:23, 25-26; 22:31-32

2 Kings 3:21; 10:3; 19:9

2 Chronicles 11:1, 4; 13:12; 18:30-31; 20:17 26:11; 32:2, 8; 35:20-22

Nehemiah 4:8, 14, 20

Psalm 35:1; 56:2; 144:1

Isaiah 19:2; 29:7-8; 30:32; 21:4

Jeremiah 1:19; 15:20; 21:4-5; 32:5, 24, 29; 33:5; 34:22; 37:8, 10; 41:12; 51:30

Daniel 10:20; 11:11

Zechariah 10:5; 14:3, 14

John 18:36

Acts 5:39; 23:9

1 Corinthians 9:26

2 Corinthians 7:5

1 Timothy 6:12

2 Timothy 4:7

Hebrews 10:32; 11:34

James 4:1-2

Revelation 2:16

CHAPTER 8

It is War Time

Throughout history, there have been a number of wars. Such as The Civil War, it was between opposing groups of citizens of the same country. Wars such as World War I and II, Vietnam, Desert Storm, and the War in Iraq were all transcontinental wars (meaning going across continents).

It is our belief that most wars do not all have a war cry. In other words, a slogan used to rally people to a cause. What we see going on right now in our country with all the unrest going on around the world should be enough to rally not just people but also the people of God, the good soldier of Jesus Christ, those who were chosen to be a soldier. Then what is going to cause you to fight?

For instance, a member of our former church was attacked in her home by a young man who had just moved into the building where she lived. Alternatively, what about the number of school shootings we have been watching on the news program or reading about online. The continued senseless killings of unarmed black men by the police repeatedly.

As many churches as we have in our local communities, should not these and other problems, rally the people of God to come together and wage war on the enemies? If our churches can get on one accord according to the Word of God we as the body of Christ can began to tear down all the strongholds that keep rising.

Therefore, when we think about wars, no war is won just by getting a group of people together and going out just fighting. However, a group of people coming together regardless of how long it takes for the plan to come into fulfillment, because being in a hurry can cause unnecessary collateral damage. God already has a planned strategy in place; all we must do is follow his plan.

For example, in the book of Joshua, sometimes we must wait in ambush. Read this:

> "And I, and all the people that are with me will approach unto the city: and it shall come to pass, when they come out against us, as at the first, that we will flee before them, (For they will come out after us) till we have drawn them from the city; for they will say, They flee before us, as at the first: therefore we will flee before them. Then ye shall rise from the ambush, and seize upon the city: for the Lord, your God will deliver it into your hand."
>
> (Josh. 8:5-7, KJV)

We find Gideon also following, God's strategy in the book of Judges:

> "And he divided three hundred men into three com-
> panies, and he put a trumpet in every man's hand
> with empty pitchers, and lamps within the pitchers.
> And he said unto them, Look on me and do like-
> wise: and, behold, when I come to the outside of
> the camp, it shall be that, as I do, so shall ye do.

When I blow with a trumpet, I and all that are with
me, then blow ye the trumpets also on every side
of all the camp, and say, The sword of the Lord,
and of Gideon."

(Judg. 16-18, KJV)

Battle Cry:

"So, Gideon, and the hundred men that were with
him, came unto the outside of the camp in the
beginning of the middle watch; and they had but
newly set the watch: and they blew the trumpets,
and brake the pitchers that were in their hands.
And the three companies blew the trumpets, and
brake the pitchers, and held the lamps in their left
hands, and the trumpets in their right hands to blow
withal: and they cried, The sword of the Lord, and
of Gideon. And they stood every man in his place
round about the camp; and all the host ran, and
cried, and fled. And the three hundred blew trumpets, and the Lord set every man's sword against
his fellow, even throughout all the host: and the
host fled to Beth-shittah in Zererath, and to the
border of Abelmeholah, unto Tabbath."

(Judg. 7:19-22, KJV)

In reading these passages of Scriptures, the conclusion was
that the people of God were victorious only after following the
plan for them. If the Church would only follow the direction of
God, then and only then will, we be prolific in all that we do.
Solomon said, "In all thy ways acknowledge him, and he will
direct thy paths." (Prov. 3:6, KJV)

After the commander and chief produces, a plan strategy and after the soldier has been trained in combat, then after coming together and getting their marching orders, then the battle cry can be given. Then we will accomplish the task before us and be VICTORIOUS. That the only way we can defeat the devil, take back what he stole and send him back to the hellhole from where he comes from.

The marching orders from Jesus were the following:

- "GO" into the hedges and highways and compel them to come."
- "If God is for us, who can be against us."
- "No weapon that is formed against us shall prosper."
- "Let this mind be in you, which was also in Christ Jesus."
- "The steps of a good man (woman) are order by the Lord."
- "Put on the whole armor of God."
- "We are complete in Him, which is the head of all principality and power."
- "Go ye therefore, and teach all nations, baptizing them in the name of the Father, and of the Son, and of the Holy Ghost: Teaching them to observe all things whatsoever I have commanded you: and, lo I am with you always, even unto the end of the world."

We have been given God's explicit directions. Now we must move forward and take back the Promised Land. God told Joshua after the death of Moses "Arise, go over this Jordan (not some of the people) but the leaders, and all the people unto the land (in Cincinnati, Cleveland, Dayton, Atlanta, Chicago, Kansas, Omaha, Houston,) which I do give to them, even to the children of Israel. (See Josh. 1:2)

Finally, the conformation that we will be successful, found in verses three and five of the chapter abovementioned:

> "Every place that the sole of your foot shall tread upon, that have I given unto you, as I said unto Moses."
>
> (Josh. 1:3, KJV)

We do not have to worry about the opposition because His word said:

> "There shall not any man be able to stand before thee all the days of the life as I was with Moses so I will be with thee: I will not fail thee, nor forsake thee."
>
> (Josh. 1:5, KJV)

IT IS WAR TIME!

CHAPTER 9

The Fight is Fixed

The Word of God says in the first book of the Bible:

And it came to pass after these things, that God did tempt Abraham, and said unto him, Abraham: and he said, Behold, here I am. And he said, take now thy son, thine only son Isaac, whom thou lovest, and get thee into the land of Moriah; and offer him there for a burnt offering upon one of the mountains which I will tell thee of. And Abraham rose up early in the morning, and saddled his ass, and took two of his young men with him, and Isaac his son, and clave the wood for the burnt offering, and rose up, and went unto the place of which God had told him. Then on the third day Abraham lifted up his eyes, and saw the place afar off. And Abraham said unto his young men, abide ye here with the ass; and I and the lad will go yonder and worship, and come again to you. And Abraham took the wood of the burnt offering, and laid it upon Isaac

57

his son; and he took the fire in his hand, and a knife; and they went both of them together. And Isaac spake unto Abraham his father, and said, my father: and he said, here am I, my son. And he said, Behold the fire and the wood: but where is the lamb for a burnt offering? And Abraham said, my son, God will provide himself a lamb for a burnt offering: so, they went both of them together. And they came to the place which God had told him of; and Abraham built an altar there, and laid the wood in order, and bound Isaac his son, and laid him on the altar upon the wood. And Abraham stretched forth his hand, and took the knife to slay his son. And the angel of the LORD called unto him out of heaven, and said, Abraham, Abraham: and he said, here am I. And he said, lay not thine hand upon the lad, neither do thou anything unto him: for now, I know that thou fearest God, seeing thou hast not withheld thy son, thine only son from me. And Abraham lifted up his eyes, and looked, and behold behind him a ram caught in a thicket by his horns: and Abraham went and took the ram, and offered him up for a burnt offering in the stead of his son. And Abraham called the name of that place Jehovah Jireh: as it is said to this day, In the mount of the LORD it shall be seen.

(Gen. 22:1-14, KJV)

People, as we look at this familiar text or passage of Scripture, we must understand that no matter what we face in life "God Will Provide" Some of you reading this even now can look at certain

58

aspects of your life and conclude that believing in God He will provide what we need.

If you have spent any time in church, during Sunday school, Bible study or a Sunday morning you are familiar with the narrative and or story of Abraham, Sarah, and Isaac. In your personal bible study time, go back to the book of Genesis chapter 18 were the lord appeared to him (Abraham) by the terebinth tree in Mamre. Upon taking notice of them, he greets them, and then had Sarah ready three measures of fine meal; knead it and make cakes. Abraham had a calf prepared and stood by as they ate. Verse nine of chapter 18 says they said to him, "Where is Sarah your wife?" He replies, here in the tent. In verse ten, Abraham is told that Sarah his wife will have a son.

In chapter 21 of Genesis, the Lord visited Sarah and the Lord did what He said He was going to do for Sarah as He had spoken.

"For Sarah conceived, and bare Abraham a son in his old age, at the set time of which God had spoken to him. And Abraham called the name of his son that was born unto him, whom Sarah bare to him, Isaac. And Abraham circumcised his son Isaac being eight days old, as God had commanded him. And Abraham was a hundred years old, when his son Isaac was born unto him. And Sarah said, God hath made me to laugh, so that all that hear will laugh with me. And she said, who would have said unto Abraham, that Sarah should have given children suck? for I have born him a son in his old age."

(Gen. 21:2-7, KJV)

Which brings us to chapter 22 immediately from the start of the chapter drama ensues. God tests Abraham and tells him to take his only son (the promised son) whom he loves and go to the land of Moriah and offer him there as a burnt offering. Abraham complies and heads out the next morning with Isaac and two young men. He went to the place where God had instructed him to go and prepared the burnt offering. On the third day, Abraham sees the place afar off, tells the two young men to stay and him and his son will return.

Is it not amazing that even though God told him to sacrifice his son, Abraham makes the statement we will return to you?

Abraham takes the wood lays it on his son, he also took the fire and the Knife causing Isaac to raise the question, where is the Lamb for a burnt offering? The story continues Abraham raises the knife, God calls Abraham twice telling him not to lay a hand on his son and that he knows that he fears God. Abraham looks up and all of sudden, behind him was a ram caught by his horns in the thicket as a substitute for the sacrifice. Did you catch that Abraham, and his wife were given a promise by God that he would bless them with a son and in doing so he tells Abraham to sacrifice this same son? In his act of obedience calls out to him to stop him and provides him a ram as a substitute to sacrifice instead of his son Isaac. Let us look at three things that can be beneficial for us.

The first thing we can take away is that we must obey God's word.

When we read these passages and the totality of Scripture that proceeds and follows it, the first thing that we can deduce is Abraham obeyed God's word.

It was in His obedience that we see through His journey, God was faithful and that His Word was a light unto Abraham's path. Simply because that is all he had to rely from the time we are introduced to him in chapter 12 of Genesis. It is in God's Word that we can find strength, can be encouraged in knowing that if God said it, we can take it that to the bank.

> "So shall my word be that goeth forth out of my mouth: it shall not return unto me void, but it shall accomplish that which I please, and it shall prosper in the thing whereto I sent it."
>
> (Isa. 55:11, KJV)

> "God is not a man, that he should lie; neither the son of man, that he should repent: hath he said, and shall he not do it? or hath he spoken, and shall he not make it good?"
>
> (Num. 23:19, KJV)

> "Ye shall walk in all the ways which the Lord your God hath commanded you, that ye may live, and that it may be well with you, and that ye may prolong your days in the land which ye shall possess."
>
> (Deut. 5:33, KJV)

The Word of God continues to say, "But be ye doers of the word, and not hearers only, deceiving your own selves." (James 1:22, KJV)

Secondly, we must understand that when we get a word from God, we can count on opposition to challenge the word God gave you.

The Bible is clear that the rain falls on the just and the unjust meaning that trials and tribulations are not based upon if you are saved or not. When we reflect on a number of things, we have endured the winds and rain that came with the storm sometimes left us with more questions than it did answers.

It was during the storm when we felt like we were unable not find an answer but Holy Spirit reminded us that we do have the answer, which is tied to the first point it is in the Word of God.

> "The thief cometh not, but for to steal, and to kill, and to destroy: I am come that they might have life, and that they might have it more abundantly."
>
> (John 10:10, KJV)

> "These things I have spoken unto you, that in me ye might have peace. In the world ye shall have tribulation: but be of good cheer; I have overcome the world."
>
> (John 16:33, KJV)

> "My brethren, count it all joy when ye fall into divers temptations; Knowing this, that the trying of your faith worketh patience. But let patience have her perfect work, that ye may be perfect and entire, wanting nothing. If any of you lack wisdom, let him ask of God, that giveth to all men liberally, and upbraideth not; and it shall be given him. But let him ask in faith, nothing wavering. For he, that wavereth is like a wave of the sea driven with the wind and tossed. For let not that man think that he shall receive any thing of the Lord. A double minded man is unstable in all his ways."
>
> (James 1:2-8)

What made me (John) shout with excitement, and what Abraham reminded us of, and what we want to remind you of is that God will provide, or God will come through. When the situation is getting the best of you, look up and look to the hills from whence cometh your help. During instances, we look back over our lives and think things over amid the storms of life just like Abraham, we can say Jehovah-Jireh showed up for your family. When the doctor said one thing, Jehovah-Jireh showed up and provided another answer. When your bills piled up and your money was, funny Jehovah-Jireh showed up and made a way out of no way. In other words, Abraham received a revelation of whom God is in our lives. He is our provider and foreshadowed what was to come.

In the book of Matthew chapter one lays it out this way:

> Abraham begat Isaac; and Isaac begat Jacob And Salmon begat Booz of Rachab; and Booz begat Obed of Ruth; and Obed begat Jesse; And Jesse begat David the king; and David the king begat Solomon. And Eliud begat Eleazar; and Eleazar begat Matthan; and Matthan begat Jacob; And Jacob begat Joseph the husband of Mary, of whom was born Jesus, who is called Christ. So all the generations from Abraham to David are fourteen generations; and from David until the carrying away into Babylon are fourteen generations; and from the carrying away into Babylon unto Christ are fourteen generations."
>
> (Matt. 1:5-17, KJV)

Thirty-three years later, another father watched his son as he laid on pieces of wood and instead of a knife and fire, a crown of thorns and was placed on His head, hammered two spikes in His wrist and one through His feet. The lamb Abraham referred to in Genesis was the lord himself. It should have been you and me on the cross, but Jehovah-Jireh stepped up and sacrificed himself so that we may have life. We can shout about the physical things God has provided though, is there anybody that still gets happy over eternal life? You know you were on your way to hell but God provided himself and because you said yes and accepted Him as your Lord and Savior, you now have a home in glory, the devil tried to throw a monkey-wrench in God's plan. (See Gen. 3) God had a ram in the bush and fixed the fight so that we can come out on the other side of the fight Victorious! On that account, it does not matter what comes your way, God has already worked it out on our behalf. Throw on your gloves, put your mouthpiece in, because the fight has started, stand on His Word and know the Lord is in the ring with us.

WORK CITED

- Strong, James. *Strong's Exhaustive Concordance of the Bible*. Abingdon Press, 1890. Print.
- Nelson, T. (Ed). 1982. Holy Bible New King James Version. Scotland: Thomas Nelson.
- https://en.wikipedia.org/wiki/Weight_class_(boxing)

ABOUT THE AUTHORS

Joseph L. Johnson was born in Cincinnati, Ohio and he is the second oldest out of a family of five. He has been married to his wife Denise for 43 years and is a father of five, Regina, Joseph, Nakwita, John and Ashlee. He earned his Bachelor's degree in Biblical Studies at Temple Bible College and Seminary and a Master's degree of Arts and Religion from Cincinnati Christian University.

John E. Johnson is a native of Cincinnati, Ohio. He is married to Larisa Johnson and they are the proud parents of five children. John is a member of Kappa Alpha Psi Fraternity Inc. John obtained his Bachelor of Science degree in Organizational Leadership and Ministry from Cincinnati Christian University.

CPSIA information can be obtained
at www.ICGtesting.com
Printed in the USA
BVHW091336030522
635996BV00057B/5483